MW00935237

Goodbye Hurt
HELLO LOVE

CHIDOZIE E. OSUWA

Goodbye Hurt HELLO LOVE.
All Rights Reserved.
Copyright © 2018 Chidozie E. Osuwa
v4.0

The opinions expressed in this manuscript are solely the opinions of the author and do not represent the opinions or thoughts of the publisher. The author has represented and warranted full ownership and/or legal right to publish all the materials in this book.

This book may not be reproduced, transmitted, or stored in whole or in part by any means, including graphic, electronic, or mechanical without the express written consent of the publisher except in the case of brief quotations embodied in critical articles and reviews.

Dreams On Paper Entertainment Publishing
https://www.dopepublishing.com

Paperback ISBN: 978-1-4787-9847-7

Cover Design by Chidozie E. Osuwa. All rights reserved - used with permission.

PRINTED IN THE UNITED STATES OF AMERICA

Contents

Chapter 1
The Peace You Deserve

You weren't stupid.
You weren't crazy.
You Weren't Foolish
You were in **love**.

—**poetic_style**

Stop ***telling*** him that you won't
put up with it, and then sitting
there and putting up with it.

—*poetic_style*

Something beautiful is waiting
for you on the other side of
this *pain*.

—poetic_style

Stop crying over a dude
who won't even raise his
hand to wipe your tears.

—*poetic_style*

Maybe you should have
stopped trying around the
same time *he* did.

—*poetic_style*

He's not ready.
And you can't **force** him to be.

—*poetic_style*

Don't stay because of how
much time you have invested.
Leave because of how much
time and hurt you will **save
yourself.**

—*poetic_style*

She doesn't want to lose what
she has with you, but don't force
her to go find it **_elsewhere_**.

—_poetic_style_

Fuck how he treated you then,
How does he treat you ***now?***

—*poetic_style*

He may have told you all
the reasons you should stay,
but his **actions showed** you
all the reasons you should go.

—poetic_style

Stop **choosing** to be naïve
because you are afraid to
do what needs to be done.
Pretending a problem does
not exist will not make it
go away.

—poetic_style

Don't let him **trick** you into
committing to him, while
he takes his time deciding
whether or not he wants to
commit to you.

—*poetic_style*

There is a man out there who
is **ready and willing**. Stop waiting
around for one who is neither.

—poetic_style

There is no such thing as
making him want you.
Either he does, or he doesn't.

—*poetic_style*

My heart wants you back
but my mind **knows better**.

—poetic_style

Too many women would rather
stay in hell, than be alone…
Don't be one.

—poetic_style

We have to learn that giving
your all does **not guarantee**
that you will get theirs back.

—poetic_style

The moment you no longer
have time for them, they begin
to **find** all the time in the world
for you.

—poetic_style

Loving someone else should
never interfere with **loving
yourself.**

—poetic_style

Dear self,

How do you expect to heal
when you keep **inviting** that
pain back into your life?

—poetic_style

Dear self,

stop falling too deep
in love with **potential**.

—*poetic_style*

Dear self,

learn to be okay with being
alone. That way you never
have to settle for anything
less than what you know
you **deserve**.

—poetic_style

Be careful.

Some men will jump through
hoops to get your time…
only to **waste it**.

—poetic_style

Walking away is
not the hardest part;
staying away is.

—poetic_style

Fire does not stop
being fire just because
you took your hand out
of the flames. If you stick
your hands back in, you
will get **burned again**.

—*poetic_style*

What if I told you that
staying, no matter what,
is **not always a sign of
strength** like some would
have you believe?

—poetic_style

Dear self,

stop allowing these dudes
to get away with doing the
bare **minimum**, and then
acting like they are the best
thing to ever happen to you.

—poetic_style

Never ignore changed
behavior and habits.
Trust your gut.

—poetic_style

Stop telling yourself that
it's not as bad as it is just
because you are terrified
of **starting over**.

—poetic_style

Be careful.

People can become someone
totally different once **comfort**
kicks in.

—*poetic_style*

Eventually,
she just got **tired** of being
a sucker for someone who
clearly didn't give a fuck
about her.

—poetic_style

The best trick she taught
herself was to treat people
according to what they
showed her.

It's ok to play games with her.
Just don't get mad when she
fucks around and runs into
a *real man* while you are
busy playing.

—poetic_style

Dear self,

Don't be the woman holding
on to **nothing.**

—poetic_style

Don't piece yourself
back together only
to hand yourself
back to the one who
broke you.

—*poetic_style*

Stop trying to force
yourself to mean
something to him
when **his actions**
have shown you
otherwise.

—poetic_style

Dear self,

maybe it's time you stop
finding new ways to forgive
the same person for the
same things, and start
finding new ways to **move on.**

—poetic_style

"…and when you see
me starting to move
on and be **happy**,
do me a favor –
leave me the fuck alone."

—poetic_style

Sometimes, you have to
choose between losing
them, and losing **yourself**.

—poetic_style

You have this idea in your
head that you can change him.
…*get rid of it.*

—poetic_style

"*Trust Me*"
says the man who
has given you every
reason not to.

—*poetic_style*

It's simple.

Sometimes, you just have to
let him go be a fuck-boy with
someone else.

—*poetic_style*

Dear Self,

Stop being so desperate for
love. It's causing you to fall
for **anything**.

—poetic_style

Stop stressing over someone
who has already started
replacing you.

—*poetic_style*

The fact that you
are still hoping for a
call or text from him
shows that you have
not decided that you
want to **move on**.

—poetic_style

Dear Self,

You weren't asking for
too much. He just knew
he wasn't on **your level**.

—poetic_style

Dear Self,

Stop giving so much of
your time to people who
have done nothing to
earn it.

—*poetic_style*

Moving on from someone
is not the same as giving
up on love.

—*poetic_style*

Dear self,

Forgive **yourself** for wasting
your time on a fuck-boy,
then move on.

—poetic_style

Let **his actions** be the
only reason you stick around.

—poetic_style

Dear self,

You already stayed longer
than you should have.
So stop looking back,
wondering **"what if..."**

—poetic_style

Sometimes,
the best thing you can
do is let them **lose** you.

—poetic_style

Keep playing games.
sooner or later, she'll
start playing **defense**.
And you'll be sitting
around waiting for a
text back.

—*poetic_style*

He had something **great**,
but he was out looking
for something good.

—poetic_style

If you stop making time
for her, don't complain
when she starts making
time for **others**.

—poetic_style

Don't let her get to the point
of "*I don't care anymore*".

—poetic_style

She's more afraid of
losing him than she
is of losing **herself**.

—poetic_style

Dear Self,

stop **chasing** after people
who don't want to get caught.

—poetic_style

Dear self,

try choosing your
own **happiness** today.
You deserve that much.

—poetic_style

Think back to the last thing
that you thought **broke you.**
Baby, this too, shall pass.

—*poetic_style*

Too many women know
that they want better,
but are afraid of **waiting**
for it alone.

—poetic_style

Dear self,

let the last time be the **last time**. He'll either learn,
or become somebody else's
problem.

—poetic_style

Don't mistake **comfort**
for love.

—poetic_style

You don't always **heal**.
Sometimes, you just teach
Yourself how to cope
with it.

—poetic_style

She wants you,
But the ***hurt*** is in the way.

—*poetic_style*

Stop putting yourself
on the backburner for
someone who doesn't
prioritize your wants
and needs.

—*poetic_style*

The harsh reality is
that you knew that
he was wrong for you,
but you chose to go
along for the ride.
Perhaps, your heart
just needed a break
from **searching**…

—poetic_style

She still loves you,
she's just tired of being
the only one ***trying***.

—poetic_style

If making you smile is
no longer a **priority**,
find someone else
who will.

—poetic_style

Stop waiting for a **fuck-boy**
to turn into a real man.
Shit doesn't work that way.

—poetic_style

There is a difference between
'accepting someone's flaws'
and 'accepting someone's
excuses'.

—poetic_style

He is not afraid of you
leaving because you have
shown him that he can
always **walk back in** at will.
So, this time, before you
shut the door, make
certain you get back all
of your keys.

—poetic_style

Be careful.
All of that "pettiness"
that you are displaying
on social media is only
showing him how
much **power** he
still has over you.

—*poetic_style*

The **reality** of who he
is may be too much for
you to handle right now,
but trust me, accepting
it could save you years
of pain and heartache.

—*poetic_style*

Isn't it a bit ironic.
she's single because
she takes relationships
seriously.

—poetic_style

Stop being loyal to people
who **refuse** to commit
back to you.

—poetic_style

Stop using love as an
excuse to be in a **miserable**
relationship.

—poetic_style

You have tried everything;
now, try **leaving.**

—poetic_style

Too many times, he has
shown you that he is
untrustworthy;
Too many times, you
have **not listened**.

—*poetic_style*

Never go back
to someone who
is ***exactly the same***
as when you left.

—poetic_style

If he's not fighting
just as hard for
you, then, baby,
he is not worth
fighting for.

—poetic_style

She's hurting now.
But she'll smile
again. All **without**
you.

—poetic_style

You keep waiting for him
to change, and before you
know it, you will get
comfortable with all of
his bullshit.

—*poetic_style*

Sometimes, she's just
a little too broken to
pretend that she's ok.

—poetic_style

Stop waiting around for answers as to why it didn't work. It was not supposed to. He wasn't the one. You are being **saved** for something better like you know you deserve.

—poetic_style

Stop letting that 'what if'
stop you from moving on.

—*poetic_style*

Let him go.

And this time, don't wait
around for him to reach out.

—poetic_style

Dear Self,

Stop sacrificing your chance at
true happiness to be in some
half ass, one sided relationship.

—_poetic_style_

Worry about getting over
him later.

Right now, all you need to
worry about is **removing
yourself** from the situation.

—poetic_style

He has already conditioned you
to tolerate a lot more than you
would have ever considered
before. Don't lose your **standards**
completely, or he'll walk all
over you.

—*poetic_style*

If he is not willing to learn
from his **mistakes**, why are
you so eager to invite him
back into your space?

—poetic_style

Stop losing sleep over someone
who did **not care** enough to fix it.

—poetic_style

Don't let anyone shelf you
until they declare that they
are ready to love you.
Live your life.

—poetic_style

Stop waiting till you are
damaged completely before
you decide to leave.

—*poetic_style*

Being single
is better than
being **half loved**.

—*poetic_style*

Love didn't hurt you;
some fuck-boy did.

—*poetic_style*

And once she gets
comfortable being
without you, you've
fucked up forever.

—*poetic_style*

She is **afraid** of starting
over because she knows
how hard 'different' is
to find these days.

—poetic_style

Being single is not the worst
thing in the world. Having to
pretend that you are happy,
while in a miserable relationship
tops that.

—*poetic_style*

Appreciate what you **learned**
from dating a fuck-boy.

—*poetic_style*

If he does not want to add
to your **happiness**, then he
should fall back, and watch
you be happy elsewhere.

—*poetic_style*

Stop making **excuses** for him
and save yourself.

—*poetic_style*

They never think that you are
serious about leaving until you
show them that you are.

—*poetic_style*

She's probably going to curse
you out, but she still wants you
to ***call.***

—*poetic_style*

She cares **too much**.
He does not **care enough**.

—*poetic_style*

Dear self,

maybe, it's time you put
a **limit** on how many second
chances you give.

—*poetic_style*

If he had made
use of all the chances
you had given him,
he would not be
in need of this
"*one more*."

—*poetic_style*

Let him go give his
half ass love to some
half ass chick. You,
my dear, are too
whole for that.

—poetic_style

You deserve a man
who is going to pour
into you **everything**
that you pour into him.

—poetic_style

Be careful what you
stay through. You are
teaching him how to
treat you.

—poetic_style

Most would have given
up on love by now.
you, my dear, are a
survivor.

—*poetic_style*

Chapter 2
The Love You Deserve

No one said that moving on
would be easy. But trust me,
the happiness that comes
later will be well **worth it**.

—poetic_style

Be with someone who does
not mind looking "*thirsty*"
or "*pressed*" for you.

—poetic_style

She **values** the things that
you don't have to reach in
your wallet to give her.

—poetic_style

Don't give him all of the
privilege with none of
the work.

—poetic_style

I **still believe** in a kind of love that many have yet to experience. A love that doesn't leave me questioning, but rather, makes me certain that it is where I belong.

—poetic_style

Just **be everything**
you say you are.

—poetic_style

It's simple.

Be with someone who is
sure that they want you.

—poetic_style

She needs someone who is
willing to lose the argument
to save the **relationship**.

—poetic_style

Don't let them make you feel
guilty for finally choosing
your own happiness.

_—poetic_style_

Don't jump at the first sign
of what you think is a good
thing.
People are great at **pretending.**

—poetic_style

She may be going to sleep
alone. But at least her heart
is at **peace**, knowing that no
one is out there making a
fool out of her.

—poetic_style

If they are not terrified
by **the thought** of losing you,
then you do not need to be
with them.

—poetic_style

There is a big difference
between **helping** him grow,
and **raising** a grown ass man.

—poetic_style

Save some love for **yourself**.

—poetic_style

It was never about
perfection for her.
It was about **progress**
and **effort**.

—poetic_style

If he **expects** it from you,
he better be damn ready
to give it as well.

—poetic_style

Lets play a game...
Lets see who can love
the other more.

—poetic_style

I'd rather have one great person to talk to every night, than to have several pointless conversations with temporary and **meaningless** people.

—*poetic_style*

You should
be **_celebrated_**,
not hidden.

—_poetic_style_

Don't let him string
you along on a **pointless
journey** because he knows
how much you want
it to work.

—poetic_style

She wants you to
listen to **understand**,
rather than listen
just to defend yourself.

—poetic_style

Be with a man who
does not want his forever
to start **without you.**

—poetic_style

Be **vulnerable** enough
to be loved. But **conscious**
enough to not get used.

—poetic_style

You should never try
to **convince** someone
to love you.

—*poetic_style*

You deserve someone
that you don't have to
share with everyone else.

—*poetic_style*

Be very careful with
who you give your
heart. They have the
power to break you

—poetic_style

Treat him according to
his *effort* and *actions*.

—*poetic_style*

Be with someone who
picks you up before you
ever even hit the ground.

_—poetic_style_

You deserve someone
who will stop at nothing
to get you, and then stop
at nothing to **keep you**.

—poetic_style

She knows that, someday,
someone will come along
and make her forget all
about you.

…she is **impatiently waiting**
for that day to come.

—poetic_style

Be with someone who's
favorite place to be is
next to you.

—poetic_style

Stop putting so much trust
in a man who has shown
you little to **nothing.**

—poetic_style

She wants someone
who has a healthy
obsession with her.

—poetic_style

Consistency is a
two way street.

—poetic_style

Be with someone who
understands that
choosing you means
giving up **everyone else.**

—poetic_style

A good man can't find
you if you keep allowing
a bad one to stand in
the way.

—poetic_style

Be **stingy** with your
time and **careful**
with your heart.

—*poetic_style*

Show me a man who
thinks you are **too much**,
and I'll show you a man
you shouldn't waste
your time on.

—*poetic_style*

GOODBYE HURT, HELLO LOVE

Her type of love
isn't **ordinary**.

—poetic_style

Stop pushing your limit
of how much fuck-shit
you will **tolerate.**

—*poetic_style*

It's so beautiful when
the excitement is *mutual.*

—poetic_style

Stop expecting a forever
type of relationship with
everyone you meet.

Some relationships will
simply **expire**.

—poetic_style

You deserve that
"*rushing home from
work to be with you*"
kind of love.

—poetic_style

Be with someone who
wants to involve you
in **everything.**

—*poetic_style*

Make sure he is either
all the way in, or all the
way out.

—*poetic_style*

It is called ***"loyalty"*** when
It is reciprocated. Otherwise,
It is called ***"stupidity".***

—*poetic_style*

Keep your guard up until
his **consistency** knocks
it down.

—poetic_style

Be with someone who
Fights to **keep you**, rather
than fights to get you back.

—poetic_style

You deserve the kind of love
that brings out the best in you
each and every day… not the
kind that keeps you
wondering how much longer
you can hold on without
falling apart.

—*poetic_style*

Choose a man who
is never "not in the **_mood_**
for you".

—_poetic_style_

Be with someone who you
don't have to convince how
lucky they are to have **you.**

—*poetic_style*

He had the power to **break** her,
but he chose to **lift** her.
That's love…

—poetic_style

She wants to feel like your
favorite song that you love
to sing.

—*poetic_style*

Don't step down to give
him a chance;
Force him to **step up**.

—*poetic_style*

You deserve someone that
gives you the kind of comfort
and security in them that
you do not have to **wonder**
if they are respecting you
and the relationship when
you are not around them.

—poetic_style

You deserve someone who
makes being faithful to you
look *easy.*

—*poetic_style*

You deserve to be happy;
with or without him.

—_poetic_style_

You deserve someone
who is always looking for
new ways to love you.

—poetic_style

The kind of love that your
heart yearns for is not a myth.
It exists. Don't let these watered
down men make you feel
crazy for wanting it.

—*poetic_style*

Be with the man who not
only wants to put a ring on
your finger, but a **crown** on
your head as well.

—*poetic_style*

Chapter 3
The Man You Deserve
(He Said)

"I'm in love with your **flaws** and everything else that makes you perfectly you."

—*poetic_style*

"I want to make you
appreciate every relationship
before me that **failed**."

—poetic_style

"I never told her that
I was different. I didn't
have to. *I proved it*."

—*poetic_style*

"I decided that I wanted
to be a **better man** before
I even approached her."

—poetic_style

"…and the sound of
her voice quickly became
my favorite song."

—_poetic_style_

"I want to give you the **kind of love** that most don't even believe still exists."

—poetic_style

"I don't have time to
cheat or do anything
else that would require
me taking a break from
loving you."

—poetic_style

"The **last thing** I want
to do is give you a reason
to give up on me."

—poetic_style

"I wake up missing you…
even when you are laying
right **next to me**."

—*poetic_style*

"If I'm going to be angry
and annoyed at someone
every damn day, for the
rest of my life, I'd rather
it be **you**."

—poetic_style

"I prayed to God for
a woman who is
everything you are."

—*poetic_style*

"You are bad for me…
in the sense that you
are **all I think about**."

—poetic_style

"I'm ok with you being broken. I want us to work on us **together.**"

—*poetic_style*

"I would much rather
lay *alone* than lay with
someone who isn't you."

—*poetic_style*

"My only nightmare is
losing you."

—poetic_style

"I tell you that I love you
everyday because I know
you like to hear it.
…but I **show** you that I love
you everyday, because I know
you need to **feel it**."

—poetic_style

"…and everything could
be falling apart; as long as
I still have you, I'm **ok**."

—poetic_style

"You showed me the
beauty in being *vulnerable.*"

—poetic_style

" **Loving you** is out
of my hands. My heart
stopped listening to
me the day I met you."

—poetic_style

"You are the upside
to anything that's going
wrong in my *life*."

—*poetic_style*

"I don't care if anyone
else understands why
I'm with you. I do, and
that is **all that matters**."

—poetic_style

"I want to spoil you
with *love*, *support,*
and *loyalty*."

—*poetic_style*

"I want to be your
heaven on earth."

—poetic_style

"You walked into my
life and introduced me
to **forever**."

—poetic_style

"Even when we spend
the day doing nothing,
it means **everything** to
me… because it's you."

—*poetic_style*

"I'm looking forward
to the **memories** we
are yet to make."

—poetic_style

"I go back and read over
our texts when I think of
you. Because living
those **moments** just once
isn't enough for me."

—*poetic_style*

"first, we fell in love
with each other.
then we fell in love
with **the way we
love** each other."

—poetic_style

"…and even when I'm
angry with you,
I'm still uncontrollably
in love with you."

—*poetic_style*

"I want to give you
the kind of love
that **rescues you**
from everything."

—poetic_style

"The thought of you
is *my safe place*."

—*poetic_style*